Unlikely Rubbish

Harley Grant

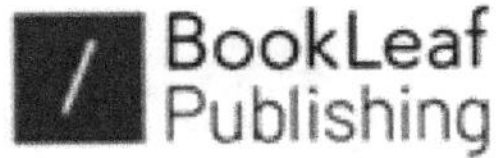

Presentation by *BookLeaf Publishing*

Web: www.bookleafpub.com

E-mail: info@bookleafpub.com

ISBN: 9789358738261

First edition 2022

Exhibition

The ravings of the mad –
dirty greasy undesirables
writhing foaming at the mouth –
sprayed in stolen hues
on back alleys,
carved into wooden posts –
a language of touch
unknowable to the
likes of you or I –
are here collected,
transfigured,
and framed for display.

Revelations of the
street-born –
street re-born
prophets of the
beginning and the end –
metamorphosed –
and sanitized for good measure –
into fine art
for the despots –
to whom the originators
of these pieces
are become invisible.

And not a penny
makes its way
to their pockets –
the for-seeing,
the peripheral
tangential tangent,
the source of all and nothing
at once –
where it might fall
through holes
worn or ripped
by the experiences –
drug fueled, erratic, wholly holistic –
of an emancipation
inherent in all who truly live
that serve to fuel
the ravings of the mad –

Frozen

Our bodies
held in stasis
a moment locked
in cryogenic tension
and our lips
so close together
so far apart that
if I inhaled
even slightly
we might collapse into an embrace.
Though I cannot
catch my breath
in hateful frost.

Our eyes
locked in fear
that darting away
might break this
icy spell.

How I ache to kiss
your lips
your neck to
free my hands
to wander about

your familiar body
in unfamiliar territory
and to know
your thawing warmth.

But I surrender
to the permafrost
that numbs my skin
and brings to standstill
my heart.
Lest I lose
the bon ami of winter
for a chance
at spring romance.

Discovery

5

She is an heiress to a legacy
of stubbornness and grandiose self worth
exchanging herself exceptionally
leaves her not a trace of vision or mirth.
Completely absorbed in acquisition
a husk adorned in all her finery
becoming deaf to our opposition
to her hysterical revisory.
Auctioned in the marketplace of entropy
chaos alone manifests her destiny.

Words

Rise up with your
painted signs
you rebels
you conservationists
you drinkers of $30 cups of joe
and demonstrate
your support
or absolute contempt
of the written word
whichever this
picket fence
picket line
of Friday morning activists
stands for.
Cry out that you
will never let them silence you
from rapping crude
and declaratively
of your love of
the sorts of sex acts
formerly only seen
in back rooms in Amsterdam,
but they can be damned sure
that you'd rather your children
become illiterate

than see the N-word
written in Huck Finn.
Some lines are not to be crossed.

It is a herculean undertaking
to preserve
or destroy
or profess to do either
that requires more
interference
then your lunch group
can handle.
But know this:
words are harmless
and revolutionary
they can make kings
and terrorists
they are dreams
and to edit
and rewrite them
one thousand times over
does nothing to change
the passions behind them.
For better or worse.

A Drunken Ramble After One Too Many - Rewritten

I need a smoke.
To keep my hands busy,
my mouth busy,
my mind off your hands
and your mouth.
I only smoke when I drink
and tonight I am drunker
than I've ever been in my life.

You sit across from me,
nursing a beer and
talking about a writer
who blew his brains out,
leaving stories splattered
against a concrete wall.

I am in love.
In love with your words
and your body.
I long to trace the scars and ink
that mark where
you've pulled yourself together
time and again.

You tell me how
girls only ever want
to fix you
and I'm confused.
How could they look at you
and see something broken?
But I can't focus
on that for too long . . .

I am drunker than I've ever been,
drunk enough to tell you
all of this,
a rant growing longer
and still not managing
to express what it is that
I am truly feeling.
Our eyes meet,
and I know
I am more in love than I've ever been in my life.

A Knot

Within a story carried by the wind
lives a lad who can speak to the sparrows,
and I recall how the bird-talker grinned
when I asked if he could take my sorrows.
He gathered them up in his palms,
then he skipped them 'cross the sea
but he must have thrown them too hard,
'cause they all came back to me.

Parallel

You could have stayed here
and gotten a job at the
hardware store with the

Help Wanted sign that's
a little more yellow each
time you pass through town.

You could have married
the girl with the big eyes who
only ever saw

you for what you could
have been, and never who you
were in the moment.

But you pretended
not to see those big eyes fill
with tears when you told

her that those who need
help are the last people who
should try to give it,

and climbed on that bus
to nowhere
leaving behind thoughts
of what might have been.

Mutiny of the Fates

Mutiny of the Fates
brought on by
nothing less than
the dissemination
of previous works
the searing stroke
of bare wire structures
warped into the
tapering shapes
of breasts and
interlocking clavicles
and serenity withheld.

That could –
were they exposed
in just the right light –
inspire a sense
of all encompassing mercy –
which would be
proportionate to
each and their
capacity for such a
truly wretched thing –
and under forced reflection
produce a necessary moment of clarity

regarding reality and your place
amongst the vastness
of cataclysmic beings.

This fragment of humanity
reflects the very idea
of victory
as can only be understood
as gradients of withdrawal,
and will be displayed
for offending glimpse
by the public eye
until its terminal debut
upon which time perhaps
the credibility of these claims
will be vindicated
and dismantled
and all flaws laid bare.

Drinks With Friends

You'll send texts to your exes
at the counsel of Gin,
but wait after a Beer
for the self-loathing to begin.

If you don't care for a lager
you might meet a nice Rum,
who'll sweep you away
for a beach holiday,
but throwing up in the bins
is the more likely outcome.

Whiskey's good for a while, but don't
invite his brother
they'll argue oe'r nationality
and who cheated on whose mother.

Then there's Bailey and Brandy,
who will serve to remind you
of girls you'd once known –
but with company only
a corkscrew away
you needn't fear drinking alone.

Analogistic

A promise, broken,
is about as useful
as a flower crown
to the owner of
a beat up truck
stalled on a back road,
as beautiful as it may be.

An apology, even a sincere one,
is about as useful
as sandpaper
when your glass is cracked
and leaking at the bottom,
lemonade sticking to your thighs
in the sun.

And a heart?
It's about as useful
as the last mix tape
from your lover
when you don't own
a cassette player.

Indigo

The girl with the beaded hair
brown eyes
and browner skin
gives a different name
whenever asked –
arm hanging out the window
sailing on the breeze
she turns and tells me
"it's the only way to be"
all unfiltered laughter
and blueberry dreams.

Cringe

How best to describe
what I witnessed
that night?
Were that I could
sprawl the experience
across butcher paper
to capture its outline –
the shape would resemble
the dragging
of chubby juvenile legs
down sun-heated
metal slides –
the colour would be
a combination
of the blood flow
from a hand
that possesses only 3 digits
and the winces
and shudders
of spectators to the
July 4th incident –
and the texture would
be that of
remembering
your neighbor

asked you to
feed her cat
a week ago
as you see her
pull into her driveway.

How best to describe
what I witnessed
that night?
Were that you could
taste the affair –
the overwhelmingly
sour notes
of angry wasps
pressed into a juice
legs still twitching
would amplify
the bitter
flavour of what
at first seemed to be
chocolates
but were revealed
rather dramatically
to be laxatives
over which they were poured –
served with a
glass of your 6th grade
teacher's sweat
from stripping

to afford supplies
and garnished with the inability
to get an erection
for a month
after you accidentally called her mom
. . . again.

Bluffing

Were I an artist
I might attempt
to replicate
the look of confusion
that graced the face
of the gambler
who saw me kissing you –
Were I a writer
of any skill
I might endeavour
to describe
how his voice cracked
and he showed his hand
when you announced
that your wife had arrived.

Finding Commonality

"It's statistically
unheard of!" said one fellow
to the other,

"To meet someone who shares
in such rarified of tastes,
and since we are both
searching for dinner
then not eating together
would be quite a waste!"

Both proposed fav'rite
haunts where they'd found the servings
to be plentiful,
and wondered at the odds
that they both would be cannibals!

Love Poem - Rewritten

You smell like absinthe.
That's all I can think
blood pumping in my ears.
I can't tell you that of course
with your cock in my mouth.
Don't throw up.
My gaze drifts
to the woman on screen –
beautiful chestnut eyes
and an ass I'd kill for.
And I'm dragged
back into the moment
when I start to choke.

I climb atop you,
unsteadily,
for a break
and to swig back whatever's on hand.
The man on screen,
not as lovely as you,
cums - O face at the camera,
but you're too high
to join him in the moment.
I'm nodding out
so I can't hear your whispers

and moans,
already knowing I'll go back
to this moment -
rewrite it,
romanticize it,
as I touch myself later.

Making Light of This

25

You're as devoted a lover
as one could hope to find,
only, there is one little thing
I can't get off my mind:
I couldn't care where you finish
but this I won't deny,
when you fret o're making bastards
it always leaves me dry.

Scarlet

She could have slept forever
amidst the bright red flowers,
had they abandoned her
as they had The Lion.

Who may not have found
his courage,
but must have found his pride,
in dreams of tearing apart
those who left his side.

"How strange it all is!"
That ruby petals
no bigger than her lips
could take down such a beast.

And that such resolution
should be found
in the likes of the smallest mice
not straw or metal men.

A Love Like That

The twinkle
in the eye
of that drunken native girl, who
while waiting
for her train
asked strangers "are you in love?"
shone brighter
and with more
purpose than any fading star.

The silence
that filled each
and every crevice of the
station when
she asked us
broadcasted your feelings clearly
to ev'ry
one except
the swaying beaming romantic
who declared
her intent
to a so often ironic universe:
"I want I love like that."

Trending

This announcement is for public safety
in response to a recent casualty
we thank the media for their accordance
as they treat this with all due importance:
please know at no time is it opportune
to attempt to dress up a wild raccoon.
Raccoons do not enjoy being attired
and this Tok Tok craze must be retired –
they use their sharp claws to get untangled
and already 12 teens have been mangled.
We understand they'd look cute in sweaters
but the cost shouldn't be the lives of trendsetters,
and under no circumstance should you feed
them peanut butter then wrap them in tweed
with a tiny bow tie and bowler hat
although what could be more darling than that?
If you really feel you can't ignore this trend
we suggest that you adopt a cat instead.

Loneliness

Loneliness is a form
of intoxication
so forgive my
isolation-soused text –
sent at 2 am
when I said
you could do better
than a girl like me
(true)
but you could also do worse
(probably true) –
I hadn't seen a soul
in days
and that had
got me pissed –
and well, I guess I hoped
you might be
half as seclusion-drunk
as I was in writing this.

Unlikely Rubbish

Small
and shitty –
some things are meant to be done that way.
No need for Broadway,
these were custom fit for the WPA.

Tickets, ripped
and pressed between flowers,
for B movies
that hold a place in your heart –
no blockbuster could ever.

The misfires, washouts, flops,
lemon scented
lead balloons
that fly into our dreams –
the sorts of treasures
to be found
in so much unlikely rubbish.